Present Infinitive

Present Infinitive

Poems by

Paul Bone

© 2022 Paul Bone. All rights reserved.
This material may not be reproduced in any form, published,
reprinted, recorded, performed, broadcast,
rewritten or redistributed without
the explicit permission of Paul Bone.
All such actions are strictly prohibited by law.

Cover design by Shay Culligan
Cover art by Gabriel Meinert

ISBN: 978-1-63980-190-9

Kelsay Books
502 South 1040 East, A-119
American Fork, Utah 84003
Kelsaybooks.com

for Heidi

Acknowledgments

My thanks to the editors of the following publications, in which these poems appeared, many in earlier versions.

The American Journal of Poetry: "Poem"
Best American Poetry Blog: "Old-Fashioned Love"
Birmingham Poetry Review: "The River," "Apologies," "Ozark Pastoral," "Asphalt," "Christmas Duck"
The Cape Rock: "Recurrences"
Cherry Tree: "Red-Winged Blackbird"
Connotations Press: An Online Artifact: "As the World Turns," "Gnats," "Hymn," "Leavings"
Ducts: "Gun Cabinet," "The Truest of Our Offerings"
The Evansville Review: "The Flaying of Marsyas"
Gracious: Poems from the 21st Century South, Texas Tech 2020: "Poem"
The Hopkins Review: "And the Elder Shall Serve the Younger"
Midwest Review: "Pallbearer's Privilege"
Peacock Journal: "Dispatch from the Gulf," "Trying to Refuse to Lament," "Compensation"
Poets Reading the News: "Even Here"
The San Diego Reader: "APGAR," "Daughter," "Present Infinitive"
Southern Poetry Review: "Mississippian," "Revenant"
Sycamore Review: "Killing the Mole"
Think: "Making the Banjo," "Leavings"
The Valparaiso Review: "Hanging the Ceiling"

Contents

Dispatch from the Gulf	13
And the Elder Shall Serve the Younger	14
Mississippian	17
Red-Winged Blackbird	18
Asphalt	20
Gun Cabinet	22
Revenant	24
One Heaven	26
Hanging the Ceiling	27
I Talk with My Brother from a Tampa La Quinta	28
Killing the Mole	29
The River	30
Present Infinitive	32
Ozark Pastoral	33
As the World Turns	36
A Nest in the Webbed Hand	38
Leavings	40
Christmas Duck	41
Poem	42
The Moths	45
Old-Fashioned Love	46
The Other Couple at the Villa Il Crocicchio	47
Medusa	53
On the Current Zombie Metaphysics	54
The Flaying of Marsyas	56
Renku: Leaks from the Deep State	57
Gnats	60
Compensation	61
Making the Banjo	62
The Shoes	65
APGAR	67
Daughter	68

The Truest of Our Offerings	69
Hymn	70
No Man's Land	71
Apologies	73
Even Here	75
The Feeling	76
Recurrences	77
Bells	79
Trying to Refuse to Lament	80
Pallbearer's Privilege	81

Dispatch from the Gulf

It's different, brothers. I'm not sure you'd like it.
No maples down here like the ones you still
have with their leaves turned backward-pale in storms.
No herons, either, standing in the fields
like Chinese vases hollowed out of slate,
magic birds sent into the land of prose.
The roads are roads like any other, cows
likewise except they share the pasture
with egrets set among them like foot lights.
Palm trees and sea grapes common furniture,
not corn. The oaks stay green all winter.
Imagine that, no seasons. No relief
from life, this setting too much like a setting.
Surely a trick will be revealed, I think,
as pelicans pass by like fleets of anvils.
It looks like paradise, but how long could
you manage to be happy? Stevens asks
if in that place there is no change
and in the asking doesn't seem to want it.
Sometimes I lift a palm leaf just to see
the scissor markings or a tracing line.
I sit all day and wait to see one fall.

And the Elder Shall Serve the Younger

And I remember now
how it nearly happened,
my brother's drowning.

We'd put on stocking caps
and walked stiffly down the road
toward the gravel pit

in our rubber boots, doubled-up socks,
and duck-brown coveralls,
our uniforms of men.

A hard freeze after sleet
had glazed the mounds of gravel
and sand into ziggurats

which held their shapes even
as we stood on their crests
now leveled and grooved where

the loader's bucket had drawn back,
dragging its teeth to prepare
a place of sacrifice.

The black boom of a crane
loomed over the quarry pond,
but it was not out there,

under the milky green
with the catfish, where my brother
descended almost to death.

Beside each of the mounds
was a pit, deep enough
to drown in we couldn't say,

the water in them so brown
and thick it was more a medium
for mud than anything.

He'd made it to the middle
of one before the ice gave way
and he dropped to his armpits,

eight years old and sinking.
All I could do was punch my way
to him, breaking the crust

and muscling through the slurry
to bring him back with me
to the shore, both of us

effigies about to become
icons in our suits of muck
already hardening

around our bodies. Back home,
we laid it all outside the door
and, when it had frozen solid,

leaned ourselves against the house
to think about the life
we missed, the one our mother

glimpsed later when the sweep
of her headlights revealed
the empty coveralls standing on their own.

Mississippian

Once the plows had turned over
last year's corn stobs, they lay
tumbled like bad teeth
in the field's dark mouth.
Among them, arrowheads and knives,
the rarer axes, and castoffs
knapped centuries ago
shined unmistakable
as a friend's face among strangers
or the white shock of potatoes
spade-cleaved and brought to light.
It was to discover that your life
was not your own after all,
to find such a thing out there
on the hills above bottomland,
the prison farther out by the river
with its rolled-wire fences,
the fertilizer tanks like downed moons
and the great skeins of snow geese
gone for the year.
To hold the smooth cool stone
in the hand—*ubi sunt*—and hope
to conjure the crossed leather lashings
that held them to ash handles,
to think of the knapper himself
wrapped in a foul wet hide,
sullen in his crouch,
the rain drumming around him
as he chipped dreams
from a common stone
and lit a door in the dark
with even these his daytime sparks.

Red-Winged Blackbird

It wore the flushed chevrons
on its shoulders with no sense
anything was wrong, bauble
pulled half-done out of the forge.
See it perch on the cattail
like a species of god-stricken
who cannot dress down enough
for this chapter on the common pond.

Behind the abandoned Walmart,
it swept the runoff ditch
back and forth and sent notes
clattering through the culvert pipe
before lighting on the reeds
saying here is water here
is water and here the willow
here the nest in the crook
and the blue eggs in the nest.

Badge splashed on at the last minute,
what of that, and why, and how?
A joke, to show us once and all
there really was no poetry
in the fields or stunted river,
only grain dust above the combines,
detergent runoff down the creeks
streaking the water like a batter.

Like water down a pipe
was how its song went, down and then
back purling up the reed and staff.
It might save you, the sound. Let it.

See the bright patch not as ornament
but a window high up in the darking
where in the proper light you see
the picture of a story.

Asphalt

We do not need a labyrinth or bay
where gods rise shining from the water
to toy with us. We have the asphalt plant
above the river, glittering black mounds
contained in stalls like mulch or excess grain,
or an obsidian vein crushed to dust.
We fear someday it might run down the banks
and turn the river into road, which was
the founders' wish at first. And when
that didn't happen they abandoned it.

In summer the commissioner of roads
stands by the asphalt and guides the county truck
back to the mounds, holds up his hand to stop them.
While it's still cool, the men inside drink coffee,
feeling the engine idle and the shocks
give when the front-end loader pours a measure
into the bed, in which the asphalt smokes
as they drive, searching for potholes to fill.
It isn't always an unpleasant smell,
the soft, hot oil just this side of fire.
Someone outside this early watering
tomatoes or holding a bathrobe closed
while bending for the paper might remind
herself to be industrious or at
the very least not mock her husband
at breakfast and in front of the children.

The holes keep coming back. The only way
to stop them is to lay a new road down—
scrape off the old one, grind it up again
above the river at the plant, then pour
it back on the naked scar and roll it flat.

Not enough workers in the world for that,
and anyway the capitol up north
would never deign to help us out down here.

We do not play at fools, like Sisyphus.
Better to roll these small stones up a hill
than get behind one that will likely crush us.

It is a somewhat mournful time of summer.
The lone white pickup with the tailgate down
going so slowly through the neighborhoods
reminds us of the cut fields east of town,
the still-green bales of hay rolled up in sleep,
the mowing an act dividing light from dark
as the earth tilts us closer to the fall
and shadows spread from the bales to overtake
the fields, where in the coolness we smell summer
rising, drifting away from us like water.
Soon it will be the August grasshopper
exploding at our feet as we shuffle
across the stubble leaving clouds of dust.
But for now what was green still keeps its green,
even if tiger lilies in the ditches
signal the end in their own nodding way.
The workers in their lime vests tamp the patches
to level them, like a dentist at a tooth.
Come winter, we will swerve to miss the holes.

Gun Cabinet

Felt-lined, soft-looking as a pelt inside,
guns lined up with their barrels
rested in the scallops of the brace board
like a docent's cared-for clutch of iron.

He'd built the doors with pointed glass
so you could see them shut up
but the little latch and key were only
decorations like on a girl's diary.

Shotgun, rifle, shotgun, pellet gun,
all down the line like that, and below
in a drawer the shells and cartridges
rolled like grapeshot in the hold.

He scribed the layout of the scrollwork
on the molding and skirting
freehand with pencil and coffee can,
then jigsawed out the Fibonacci curves.

Just lumberyard pine, soft and buttery,
easy to dent but pliant in its
surrender to the sanding block,
any divots wetted so to rise

like welts and be smoothed down,
then the whole thing stained
to look like other wood, walnut,
wiped of its excess and shellacked

and rubbed to a matte gloss
with fine steel wool. The felt
was the last thing, the backing,
the something else inside to take

the weight of the blued steel
with grace, a reminder
of something we could not quite say
but kept in front of us all anyway.

Revenant

The grass was green, the house empty,
I thought—no truck in the driveway
as I walked up, but then to find
my brothers in the kitchen shocked
as I was at the clock alarm going off
and his tall, naked form laid out
on the bed as if he'd come home
for lunch, taken a shower,
and fallen asleep. We let him rise
then on his own, put on his clothes,
and talk to the friend on the job
he had to head back to—forms
to pull from footings, another bedroom
to frame in, some kid always late
and even this did not anger him,
just going about it all as if he still
had business here, talking patient
as before. By the hall mirror we saw
him lace his boots, buckle his belt,
and put on his shirt, all the while
whoever it was still on the other end.
If he noticed us, he had the grace
not to say so nor turn to look,
for we were all stunned to silence,
worried our noisome breathing
might scare him off too soon.
He looked in the mirror a last time,
stuck a pencil under his hat band,
and walked past us out to the truck
that maybe now was here for him,
we guessed, though we heard no door,

no engine that first warm morning
to tell us he was gone, only
the aftersound of his voice, as when
from far off the roofer's hammer
sounds the nail not as it falls but rises.

One Heaven

Smell of lake water, outboard exhaust.
Moss on the boards, carp passing
like orange ghosts under the dock.
Chigger-pocked hips squeaking
on the gunwales, and somewhere
a cooler bonking closed
as the soul is put on ice.

Hanging the Ceiling

He'd hoist a panel to the ceiling
and have me hold one end,
keeping his head dead center,
and stand there like a pillar.

Then pluck a black nail from his mouth
and drive up his two corners,
gypsum dust sifting down
as if from small detonations.

Deliberate as a man walking ice,
he turned and slid an elbow
to take my end, face whitened now
as a wraith, the hammer rising.

Four strikes and the nail was in
and countersunk in its quarter-sized dimple
where later he'd knife in the spackle
then mud and tape the joints.

For now he'd hung a kind of screen
over the wiring of heaven,
a hole cut here and there
through which the lesser light would dangle.

Outside was darkness, early winter.
The tripod lights shone up at his work
from the corners of the room
as the dust sank through our rising breath.

I Talk with My Brother from a Tampa La Quinta

He calls from Iowa. It's late or early,
I'm not sure. I listen for a darkness.
He talks about dogs, how they won't
fuck off but cats will. He asks me
to sing opera, which I can fake
in a rich baritone. We used to do
impressions of uncles, actors,
and estranged family friends
to entertain the Thanksgiving audience.
His voice is deep over the line, deeper
than mine though I try to match it.
Code switching is what they call it,
an effort to resolve dissonance,
make different things sound the same.
Listen how Iowa and Florida
sound good together right there.
I tell him about the manatee I saw,
dark oval with a head attached
out in the river. It looked like it could sing,
or wanted to. Then its head went
underwater. They had a sign
for manatees and one for alligators.
Be scared, but not too much, I think
was the point. I hear his friends
leave the bar. A door closes. His lighter clicks.
It's cold up there, I remember.
He doesn't speak. He may be listening.
How long before I ask him if he's there?

Killing the Mole

Noon breaks and it's my father in a lawn chair.
I cannot tell the difference between his shirt
and the chair back's weft and warp.
He almost isn't there. Across his lap
the spade at rest, grease shining on the blade.
How does he know the mole will show itself
just now, at this hour? He sits. He smokes a cigarette.
I try to feel the air on my left side out there.
It's just enough to pull the smoke away.
His loneliness feels good and makes him patient.
The tufted, patchy grass of unmown April
seems to wait with him ritually.
And then he leans so slightly forward
he may not have moved at all. Dark earth, dug-moist,
comes up in crumbles in front of him.
Faster than I've ever seen him move
he's up and scooping out the mole.
It flips, lands, and waddles on its outsized paws,
pink star of its nose sniffing for home,
the claws digging at air as my father comes on.
The spade goes up and comes down on its neck,
and then a flash of red so quickly made
at first I do not know what's happened,
as if a door was opened on some shame
about to rise until the boots step bone
by cracking bone to flatten it.

The River

It collects a toll of jugs and bags,
dishwater rags and collar bones.

It lowers and thins from brown to green
so you see the little shoes.

They point to the park upstream
then swim off and forget to stay.

The current drags all the johnboats south
where a mouth or a drain sucking slow

twirls round once and all the bloated carp
like a carousel now winding down,

while the catfish hunker underneath like monks,
siltwise and drunk and past time.

You'll never hear a barge full of coal,
the call of the horn round the bend,

nor see the moon of the tugboat's light,
the shrug of its wake passing by.

But you, you, and you, you could all go down
to the cottonwood backwater sloughs,

where the gar deny all treble hooks
and the cook attends to his meth.

Down there you might think of the town itself,
that it was one time meant to be.

But the river floats no traffic now
save for coffins, light, and foam.

And the heron's secret rookery?
What should we say of that?

Each turn you make floating down
the heron tows you on, out of sight.

Present Infinitive

He come up to the house the other day
is what we'd say, a persisting present tense
of arrivings never leaving that other day,

a slip of usage, less important, say,
than slipping fan belts or a fading sense
that I come up to the house the other day.

A well-greased come-along might make me stay,
the clicking gears aligning post and fence,
arriving, never leaving that other day.

On the steps I scraped my boots free of their clay
and clapped them twice together. Here are hints
I come up to the house the other day.

The door sticks crooked in its frame. In its way
it tells me where but never quite the when
arriving, never leaving that other day.

I checked the shed for tools and their intents,
the saw's division and the hammer's dents.
I come up to the house the other day
never arriving, leaving that other day.

Ozark Pastoral

I don't know any more than you
what the ewe's name was, if
she even had one. Agnes? Virginia?
But the story goes that Philip
the buck ram muscled in around
the trough and slammed her so hard
into the burred corner it opened
her shoulder down to slick white bone.

It took his mother and his brother
and him to talk his father out
of loading the squirrel gun
and shooting her behind the wool shed.
He told me this. He pleaded, said
he would care for her in her lameness.
And how they saved her was this.
They took the top course of cording
from a feed sack and threaded that
through their mother's quilting needle.

What happened next is something
close to what you might believe.
He had his brother hog tie her
while he set himself up behind
so she wouldn't kick his guts out
while he attended with patience
and a little coldness to closing her wound.

Then they splashed corn whiskey
down in the bleeding gash and dabbed
the clotted gore from her wool to see
where in the skin to run the needle.

I still don't know how you can hold
a creature down like that and stitch
it up as you might patch a quilt or
draw a curtain over secrets.

Another story is my grandmother's
mother liked taverns and sawyers
and said fine when my grandfather
came along and took away this
younger of her daughters,
a fourteen-year-old mouth to feed.
In Missouri, once you leave the pastures
and walk the timber, in canyons
no bigger than a footprint
God stamped in the damp creation clay
and left to dry, you can't see
what's going on. It's hard to know
where sounds come from.
Whether you are audience or cast
in the limestone amphitheaters.
It's a late sunrise and an early night,
a prologue, then like that a curtain call.

Reader, here's where I can say
something more or something less.
I mean about the distance between
my grandmother and this ewe, or
the ostentatious horns of metaphors.
The ewe is seventy-five years dead.

She was good. She always lambed good,
he said. She lived three more years.
But he had to mind her.

The muscle never healed straight.
She couldn't fight for her food.
He had to hold his hands out to her
so she could eat the good golden crack corn.
It was like lifting something, the strength
of hunger pushing on his palm,
even through the fine chin bone.

As the World Turns

My grandmother would say
*give me them glasses them's filthy
I don't know how you see out of these*
or *wash that apple before you eat it
some colored man at the grocery store
might have handled it.* I thought she knew
something I didn't, that I might see
the man some day with clean lenses,
hear some news of his life, his job.
Either thing she said in one register
of minor irritation, as if the pilot light
had gone out and there were no matches.
When I was there in her house,
just her and me, wind came down
the chimney, like an oracle, I would
likely say now. You had to help it
speak what news it brought. The tv
too was riddled like prophecy.
On the soaps, one minute Sarah,
recovering from surgery,
was shocked to see her twin bedside.
She disappeared in a gray scroll
of static, then transmogrified
in the kitchen, considering the knives
lined up on the magnetized rack.
They drifted through a snow,
sleepwalking their closed world—
the alcoholic insurance agent,
the nurse in her erotic blue scrubs,
the brown children skipping
down the street, singing in cities.
Why did they hide their faces?

I wondered where in a store a man
might work but never show himself.
Back with the butchers, sawing meat
in pinkening aprons and paper hats?
Their heads passed back and forth
across the portals of the swinging doors.
Back in there, maybe, he who
handled our fruit with great care,
standing alone near a bowl of it.
He washed his hands slowly, like an actor,
as if he knew he was sought for.

A Nest in the Webbed Hand

I cannot remember if it was
the middle and ring together
or first to middle and little to ring.
All the same, Uncle Bernie's hands
were a little like the chicken wings
Aunt Maxine lined up before she
dipped them in milk then rolled
them in flour to fry, looked like
wings do when plucked and raw,
as if they once did something
more. They hovered before
his face at dinner. Delicate instruments,
as you might imagine, glossy and red.
How did he hold my Aunt Maxine
in the dark? Well, you would think.
She smiled all the time. She blushed
around him. The box fan near
the stove rolled the tablecloth along
its bottom edge. It cooled the sweat
on Bernie's face. He finely buttered
a roll, the skin of his fingers
smooth as glass. I wondered,
but never asked, if they hurt at night.
Whippoorwills flew from the oak
to the gourd feeders on the porch
and back again. You heard them out
through the window, talking the way
they do under the grownup talk.

They would go on like that even as
Bernie took out his teeth at night
and put them in water, kissed Maxine,
then rose up out of bed
in the morning as the birds roosted
and hushed themselves. He held
everything nearly as you or I might,
only with a little more faith, the way
just two thin branches cradle a nest.

Leavings

The potato seated in the heel
of her hand like an infant's head,
she back-peeled with the paring knife
so that the shape she plopped
into the water was all sheared angles
and planes, its once sloped roundedness
rendered into geometry
and not a fleck of skin left on.
And in the bucket, wedges
more like than peels you could see through.
For just that time the sound
of the knife with the sound
like *edge* as it cut the milky flesh.
To ask her why she did it this way
and not use the peeler was
to ask the potatoes why
they grew underground in the first place,
only the shrug of the hills in reply,
bare fact of the pitchfork
reducing them to divots,
heap of the meaty skins later
and the water clouded in the pot,
the getting through to eating,
the blue ring of flame again.

Christmas Duck

It's simpler than you might think
to get the meat out of them,
the seven mallards and the one teal
laid across the open tailgate.

Their bodies are loose and soft,
and of course it's the emerald neck
and head of the drake you notice,
powder-blue chevron on his wings.

The heads go this way and that
as we get them square on their backs,
and as one looks off to the side
there's the faint grin of the lamellae.

Something of a knife sharpened
already inside them provides,
keel of the breastbone
you only have to find

with your thumbs then push against
to split the skin from inside
feathers and all and peel to uncase
the blood-dark engine of the wings.

It's important, later at the sink,
to clean the breast fillets well.
Sometimes a ball of steel shot
embeds a feather in the muscle.

Weeks later the image comes back,
quill in the meat, when above
the late quartets and wine murmur
a pellet tinks on someone's plate.

Poem

—for Brigit Pegeen Kelly

In this town I still say I'm from, one night
two boys played catch with a cat, a black cat.
They were the kind of boys who sewed eagles
to the backs of their denim jackets and smoked
a resinous weed with the density of a star.

It was difficult to see this cat near the end
of the dock where dark lake water caught
the cat each time they threw it in the air
and into the lake with its fuel and oil slicks
now invisible but palpable, most likely,
to the cat.   And it's truer to say they were
playing catch with the lake, because the lake
gave the cat right back to them each time,
exactly where they waited.
                          The cat was easier
to see in the water, oddly enough, than it was
in the air. A light above the fuel station
at the end of the dock glinted on its wet fur,
you see.   Otherwise you wouldn't have known
it was there, for it made no sound while it swam,
only screamed when it sailed out over the water
and into the water, where it then went silent,
a shadow swimming in a larger shadow.

This enraged the boys, who took it as an affront
that the cat did not complain, so they threw it
farther and higher each time, and each time
the cat came back, trying to find a place where
the boys were not. There was no place like that.

It might have looked as if the boys guided
the cat back to shore, as if indeed the cat meant
to get back to them.

     It wanted to get back
somewhere, a box in a basement
next to a humming furnace, most likely.

It's fair to ask why no one stopped this.
After all, I did punch one of the boys
in the face and knock him out.
       That was before
the cat, though. The timing was wrong, as much
as we'd like to believe he got his punishment
before his crime. Also, there were two of them,
one to bend down and retrieve the cat and one
to keep me away. They were bigger by then.

They may not have stopped growing, in fact.
They are giants. One of them now paints bridges.
I wish I could say a pharaoh commissioned
his work to commemorate a stone causeway
over the lower Nile, that along the bridge's span
in subtle variations he painted the fine profiles
of cats in their eternal stillnesses.
       Instead, he hangs
by a harness over the highway and covers the sides
of each bridge with green paint. He makes
a good deal of money but little sound dangling there
above traffic.
    He has shaved his head, now grown
more pointed and delicate from hours in the sun,

perhaps, or from the way we begin here to picture
him transformed into the image of the creature
he has certainly forgotten.
        You might even say
he has come to resemble, in profile himself against
the bridge in sunset light, a fine-boned pharaoh,
his skin tawny as he awaits eternity, his ears
sharp and laid back this evening, away from
his family and dangling from the overpass.
              He turns
now in the harness to watch the sun descend
to a horizon shimmering in the heat like water.

He knows it is only corn out there, but in spite
of himself he sees only a vast green lake.
As when a river still flows in a flooded valley under
the greater body of water,
        so do the cars below him.
Perhaps just now he remembers the cat, which swam
under the dock but did not appear on the other side.

The Moths

Ed Taylor was the sheriff at that time,
and one or two of us who'd made trusty
(because our mother managed Ponderosa
or, failing that, we read and did not talk back)
might wash his car on Sunday as he went
to church across the street from the grain elevators.
The principal business: seeking out
a tire fire down at Seven Oaks
or a pod of bondoed Chevelles and Nissans
marking the circle of the communal joint
as Zeppelin rattled the speaker on the cab.
So Reggie Hemsley and I filled our buckets
with diesel from the leggy tank
out by the tool shed and scoured a week's worth
of night driving from grill, hood, windshield,
sometimes the pastel corpse of a Luna moth
big as a sage leaf still caught
under a wiper blade, maybe a Clover looper
with one wing still raised, whether in surrender
or defiance who knew. The whole effect
was like the peeled hull of a whaling boat
or the moths and mosquitoes not what
they were but the scorched cowl of a craft
plowing through darkness. Then at night,
back in the cell, the huge fans going and sweat
dripping from elbow to notebook, I sketched
the corn and bean fields as outer space
and the copses around farm ponds docks
where crafts might refuel and the drivers
grab coffee or bourbon before setting out again,
the county out there not a place to be caught
but full of luminous bodies which, once
you shined a light on them, they disappeared.

Old-Fashioned Love

I would have traded buttonholes for zippers.
Would you, in love back then in sepia town?
Would you have held the bloody kerchief while
I coughed into it? We can still imagine
afflictions were a kind of lyricism,
that if you slipped a buffalo nickel
into the slotted pupil of a goat's eye
you might get back a murmur in your lungs
instead of all these shallow knifey breaths.
Allow the planet unillumined, too.
See us there like original creatures
in those days just before the streetlamps
diluted all the living constellations,
agog as every night the gods retrenched
the delta of the galaxy in colors
most like the beautiful diseased parts of us.
I'd likely now be helping you in
the little gum tree canoe I'd hatcheted.
We'd do away with pretense since the stars
bend all the way down to the lake to catch us.
We toss our straw hats on the water or
the sky and row, admiring the little infant graves
lined up along the cemetery shore,
legible even in the cedar shade.

The Other Couple at the Villa Il Crocicchio

1

Tuscany was the idea for the honeymoon.
Mornings we would walk the olive groves
and vineyards near the villa,
then take a train to Florence or Siena, maybe Arezzo.
I would think of James Wright, Dante, and my wife
would guide us through the passion paintings.
Our son hovered gravely in the mind,
left safely enough with family, so young still,
so blank yet in our life, not walking or talking.
Go on, they said. *He won't remember any of this,*
hello and goodbye all the same to him.
Still. Superstitions. Hasty marriage.
Abandonment. I calculated hierarchies of sin.
I put us on a round of terraced land peasants
once farmed and the poet repurposed
as a subdivision of iniquities.
Who thinks like that? I thought
before the thought came—
no telling yet how far down or up we'd be.

2

After the diesel smoke of the Autostrada,
after the faces of wrath in the rearview mirror
when I dawdled in the left-hand lane,
after the dwarf orange in the courtyard
with one orange hanging like a bloated moon,
especially after that, the voice was like
a Florentine's who offered at first
some brief comfort, and then dire news
of the future which was really the past,

delivered from a molten tomb
or face-down in sewage—

so clear the voice, so redolent of home,
despondent, too, nostalgia's quick vernacular.
For now, it seemed just a mystery, the voice
and its American anxiety
polite and muted in the wooded office.
Then Sonia showed us to our room, the kind
you might imagine writing letters in,
though you would not, because the news you heard
from that voice was, like the stucco and the wicker,
blank as yet, an empty hole to sink your fear in.
We unpacked our bags, a motion in
reverse, most likely, of the other couple.
Only later would the orange seem an omen.

3

That evening, with our wine and cheese poolside,
we looked across the valley where the mountain
rose, going from green to black as house lights
or torches dressed its dark side, at the top
a stone house silhouetted and likewise lit,
where I imagined Guelphs and Ghibelines
strappadoed kin and enemy alike
in shifting balances of dominance.
Then dinner, more wine, a walk around the groves,
leaves of the olives pale enough
to light a sotto passaggio
through the field then back to bed.
Our room was next to yet another couple,

minor but still significant, because
the woman moaned in time to a faint thumping
just as we either drifted off to sleep
or started to make love ourselves. At first,
especially if we were in that fall just before
sleep, it was impossible to tell if it was just
a dream, so close to not-there were her sad come cries.
And if they started as we were making love,
we felt there was no choice but to ape
the sounds our neighbors made, not to harmonize,

but more to cancel out this thing between us.
It sounded more and more like someone trapped,
the vowel she uttered nightly, tinged enough
with danger tempering pleasure that we
could not find any way to talk about it.
I wondered if their room was darkly wooded,
and if that caused her silence in daylight
when, if we saw them, the man glared at us
as if we'd wandered to close to a ditch
he meant to guard. He held her at the elbow.

4

But what of that man and his gentle voice?
We wondered the next day, talking at the bar,
the doors of the lobby thrown open to the light
so we could turn in our stools and see the grapes
across the road, the hedgerows of rosemary.
Apologizing for her cigarette,
Sonia emerged from her office paperwork
to ask if we would like a *limoncello*.

At first, she only said they were from
Minnesota. Where was Minnesota?
It's in the middle, more or less, but cold,
a little like this, though, somewhat. No olives,
some vineyards, cows, pleasant hills and people.
Yes, many farms. Common blind bag of details.
She'd grown up in the country, too, where still
you slaughter a hog in the fall and then
for two weeks render lard and set the meat
to curing, kettles roiling, many women tending fires.
She filled our little glasses again.
I'm sorry, she said, but two limoncellos
will make me talk. What of the man? we asked,
the man there in the office yesterday.
What had happened? What had, indeed, happened?
This was their last stop on a month-long tour—
Morocco, Barcelona, Paris, Zürich, Tuscany.
While riding horses near San Gimignano,
she . . . broke down in her nerves? Lost her minds?

What is the word? We didn't know ourselves.
At all events, she had to remain prone.
She lay infirm in the *Ospedale Santa Maria Nuova*.
Catatonic. Calls back to St. Paul were ongoing,
requests to the embassy for insurance, a taxi
to Rome to catch a non-stop home.
Any movement to upright terrified her.
She could not handle layovers of any kind,
no undue agitation or movement.
The parents even now boarding in Minnesota.
The way back home is always crooked.
So sad, we said. How pitiful. To think
of her rigid with fear out in the country,

riding a horse in the hills of Tuscany
like some profaned image in a travel guide.
Dante walked down a hole wound like a funnel.
The road leads on. Walk here, it says.
But then there is everything else,
the space of the darkness. I am lost.
You reach out to the damned.
They tell you who you are.

5

We thought about them often,
of course—what possible transgression
placed them here, away from home,
incapable of leaving, or of loving
one another until such time
as who knows what determines?
Were they bearing our sins for us?
We haunted churches, walked
stony paths along their sides,
stooped in the shade of alcoves.
We kept our voices to ourselves,
interrogating passion narratives,
collating pietàs until they all
layered one on the other.
The votives flickered in abdication.
The statuary was accusatory.

6

And then the last night, we saw
the husband at dinner, one half
our proxy couple, sure enough
there with her just-arrived parents
who smiled but searched dark corners
as if to find the daughter made whole.
There was the sawing of bread
from the kitchen after we ordered
Misto Toscano, the farm's chianti,
fettuccine and truffle sauce.
We listened to their conversation,
not for what they said, for the din
made that impossible, but for tone,
diagnosis, some wavering in a laugh,
a gesture, a goblet in a trembling hand,
something that might tell us
their gradation of suffering
so that we would not have to ask
because, as any resident of hell
will tell you, the present is dim
but the future hovers right there
before you if you will only look at it.

Medusa

Mad curator in the colonnades,
docent of her iterative statuary—
all young men old, pockmarked by weather,
cowls of vulture shit atop their heads,
hunters, lovers, athletes, all once distinct.
She had forgotten: had they always
been here? Had she herself perhaps
set them here to keep the thieves away?
The one she hasn't met but somehow
remembers raises his shimmer of bronze.
That's the contrapose she circles, amazed
at his powers of aversion, a knowing movement,
something he trained for. She dreams
of stone made animate, coming for her.
She retreats deeper in the labyrinth,
aware that some day, when he comes for her,
she will at least know what her warning is:
sole of a sandal rubbing in the gravel,
a sword sliding from the scabbard,
tip of it singing like the bell of time.

On the Current Zombie Metaphysics

Before the crash in late '08,
they sped up for a minute,
avaricious as day traders
bargaining away reflections
of abstractions of our mortgages.
They learned to load and shoot,
to separate into packs.
Then they slowed down, emblems
perhaps of gridlocked legislators
or laid-off drywall finishers,
dragging one Redwing
or Italian loafer behind them
in a loop downtown past
the unemployment office
or the topless bar.
Now they have nuance,
complicated provenance,
a good sense of realism.
No one says *zombie* anymore.
How quaint, as if the survivors
know and resort to *noms de mort*
like walker, infected, Subject J.
Everything a virus, a medical problem.
And then one day not, just waiting
until they starve, until the last one
crawls to the family plot.
Or worse, to the last living,
they are agents of conflict the way
adultery or money used to be.
Though that is still a problem.
We are no better, is the lesson.

The monster is here, under your palm
held against your heaving chest,
the face above the machete.
Foils, we would call them.
What choice do they have,

stripped down as they are
by radiation or pathogens
to the hindbrain, too dumb
and slow to apprehend any
but the overweight, distracted,
and the self-involved. They pray
in church to a zombie god,
which is identical to the living one.
Yet the icon, bloody and ravaged
as they themselves are,
attracts their adoration but hangs
there on the lumber and does not
acknowledge them. And still they stay,
well-mannered and quiet,
waiting for communion.

The Flaying of Marsyas

Apollo hung the goat head down
and cut to reason's bone,
the satyr's skin a dripping gown
that scholars wear alone.

Renku: Leaks from the Deep State

tell me a secret
I will there are no corners
in this room you see

I left a message
for the people of the wall
which I'm still writing

a finch in the bush
whistling of an empty egg's
sources and methods

the mother rabbit
looked all of us in the eye
bending to give birth

a grackle dying
near the eggplants turns out to be
two grackles mating

I left the shovel
stuck there in the ground like that
so the finch could perch

trumpet vine remembers
the shape of the shed—the field
does the forgetting

in the evening gloom—
sound of robot vacuum's splash
cleaning up the pool

mallard in the pool
do I still know how to play
ducks on the millpond

all week the banjo
sat there with its big moon face
near where the cat sleeps

robins call down the day
and even the red schoolhouse
turns a shade of blue

moon through clouds tonight
as Buson's wife combs her hair
you thought she was dead

my son pierces me—
"you can tell a man's dreams
by the beard he grows"

all our talking stopped—
a great blue heron flying
right over the streets

parking lot heron
quiet as a bowling pin
waiting for a strike

east on 70
pump jacks hoist the sun at dawn
it takes all of them

just the noon siren
yet in the western sky clouds
banked up like kettles

lizards dart away
like poems I meant to write
about lizards once

Gnats

Just as you shut the window, the sound
of your voice hung there as I turned to say
my own farewell. I knew I had to leave.
Before I did, the cloud of gnats between us

(well, between you, the glazing, and then me)
jumped when I spoke what you couldn't hear
then gathered again in their tightened prayer.
So many ways of telling you about them

occurred to me then. Golden molecules
aswirl in autumn light you might have liked,
a microplanet made of living motes
that pulsed in sympathy with the universe.

Synapses crackling above a spine of air
you would admire but not be touched by.
They're also only gnats, I would have said.
The ganglia take wing and not the spirit.

But still I talked to them and made them move.
I told them things I'll never say again.
Such a sight, those seething reels of light.
But you were still inside, and I was out.

Compensation

He'd come to know the pain
as a thing placed in his back
and not a true part of him.

At first it seemed wrong
to think it a visitant,
a guest of harm.

Then it changed, became
an axis he'd barely noticed
yet now stood forever tilted.

Rather than bend straight down
to pick up a sack of concrete,
he would curl around a pole

he imagined and swing
the sack up with his left side
then hoist it to his shoulder.

In this way he remained
useful, reminding himself,
where others hadn't, that his body

lived partly now in a spot
beside him, as if he were
minding someone else's pain

and, since pain defines one's story,
then that other story too,
for he had forgotten his own.

Making the Banjo

> *In America and on the Islands they make use of this instrument greatly for the dance. Their melodies are almost always the same, with little variation . . .*
> —Dena Epstein, *Sinful Tunes and Spirituals,*
>   *Black Folk Music to the Civil War*

Grow a calabash gourd
between two boards. See
how it stays nice and flat.
Hang it from the porch eaves
and shake it next spring, hear the seeds.

Now cut two holes, one on
the big bulb one on the little.
Soak your scraps of goatskin,
stretch them on over
to make a pair of eyes or windows.

Thumb the tacks on through
the skin into the meat
and make a crown of brass round it.
This will keep it still,
for skin wants to return to itself.

Take a long neck of maple,
glue a stick on its backside,
run it through the gourd.
Stretch the gutstrings
over the skins, tune to pitch.

That's the hard part.
The easy part is now
you knock out a tune.
It's an old fruit,
this head you're playing on.

It's a ship rocking in the waves,
the taut plucked rigging
sounding down in the chamber
where all the notes are laid
foot to head and the iron tone rings ring.

It makes a sound like chains
in the hold of a ship.
Call it Billy in the Low Ground
if you want, call the melody
Celtic by way of slave ship rhythm.

This is the easy part.
Hear in the downbeat
back of your fingernail,
the short high drone string
under your thumb most constant

the outcry at the whipping post.
Or don't hear it. Just as well
not to think of it
as anything but parts,
an animal, a fruit, a tree.

If torn apart then put
together this very way,
stretched and flattened and bent,
carved and cured and pierced,
they make a sound of many

that is really only one sound.
It starts as wavering,
as when the wailings
in a field rise or lower
to meet at the tonic past all pitch.

The Shoes

When she miscarried
in the office bathroom
he carried her down
the three flights
over his shoulder
in view of everyone
and noticed as he watched
his step on the flecked
granite stairs
drops of blood form
coronas on the hide
of his shoe tops.

By evening the blood
turned black the shoes
changing almost as
turned to or away
a presence flashes
or closes to a line
tying the laces
the next day rising
to shut the bedroom door
to leave her rest
that seam closing

He meant to burn them
his thought was wrong
that he could have
something else close
that might become him
the shoes simply medium

He wore them anyway
months until the blood
could not be told
from ordinary indignity
of rain and dust smoothing
the burred life of the suede
degradation of blood
he tucked them in the closet
cool dark tomb of forget
where they sat patient
waiting for their next move.

APGAR

When you were born, you didn't make a sound
until they put you on the warming table,
cold chick, bluish and mute. The reddened gowns
the nurses wore were soaked as in some fable

in which the father (please not me), on seeing
his daughter's eyelids shut against the world,
her mouth a seam the waxy vernix seals,
head a neglected fruit, the fine fists uncurled,

moves in a kind of dream. The iron tang
of blood on the elemental floor, the mother's sense
of something wrong draining her face, all hang
in some between-time as he wonders when

he'll have to tell. But then the light goes on,
blood rises under your skin, you raise your arms.
You squeeze life in your fists, you sing your song
wide open so to break the tale's dark charms.

Daughter

I glimpsed your purple backpack in the woods,
looked back and it was just the autumn leaves
flickering like fish. The pinkish hood
you took your angry shelter in, the sleeves
you pulled up to the elbow, even in cold—
all gone, only the shadow of the yew
that said I gave you up. By now I was old
and had forgotten how it happened. Clues
came and went like the seasons, more like flashes
of you—a curve of brown hair through windshield,
pile of bright bedtime books reduced to ashes,
your green voice from the corner of a field.
Whatever happened happens every day.
I haven't checked the churchyard yet. I may.

The Truest of Our Offerings

Sorry to mention the chorus of cicadas
and the constellations of fireflies
blinking where I've just looked or am about to.
Reader, do you say fireflies or lightning bugs?
It's lightning bugs where I'm from. We also
said locusts not cicadas. Likewise bats, apologies
for the entry of the bats who skim the pool
right now and yaw right back into a sky
always lighter, it seems, than it should be
for bats. Their bellies flash ochre above
the faux-Aegean tiling around the edge.
My daughter saw her first bat yesterday.
She thinks there's just the one or maybe two
in Indiana, and therefore the world, swinging
as if on wires, toy bats eating toy mosquitoes
then drawn back up somehow like props or puppets.
I have to tell her they're not bad, mosquitoes,
despite the welts and the maddening itch.
They just drink blood, the way mosquitoes do.
They keep the bats well fed and in the air.
You'd think it would be the other way around,
that she would see the bats like blood avengers,
something indeed to fear. But no, like gods
or demons, they have limits, and weaknesses,
what with the intercession of mosquitoes,
who sing them from their caves and bring
from us the truest of our offerings.

Hymn

He went every Sunday to hear her sing.
The church was small and had no choir,
only his daughter, the twin violinists,
and the piano player, all so young.
Yet they performed their services as if
they were the ushers or the cleaning crew,
with experience and routine efficiency.
Before the faithful rose for bread and wine,
she sang the four notes of the alleluias
sharply so that they were not lost the way
the chapel's echo sometimes overtook
the chaplain's voice and something of his message.
He knew the pinging of her vowels was practice,
that even though she might have still been moved
by her own voice, it was in her forgetting
herself that made it ring against the stones
and moved the congregants to take communion,
if one thing could be said to move them so,
as it so often moved him years ago
to leave his chair and follow down the hall
the source of that voice, which of course he knew
but only wished to see and hear again—
her back turned to him in the bedroom, not
from anger but because she might be lost
rearranging the family in the dollhouse
or putting on pajamas after showering,
her hair still damp and darkening the shirt,
which she ignored or, more precisely, didn't notice,
so busy was she singing to the people.

No Man's Land

So far my son has the furniture of collapse
ready to go—disrupted power grid,
reavers and highway robbers tearing down
what's left of all the playhouse plans of grownups.

I listen as he works. Halting, quiet.
He's at the map like Caesar, staring at the wall.
He sequesters us with his red marker
into nation-states who constantly destabilize
each other after a series of secessions
set us all against each other once again.

But there's a problem. There's no story yet.
He's stuck between ideas and movement.
Say for instance the recruits for this province
have gathered in the gym where years ago
their parents ran up and down the court,
the bleachers long ago stripped for firewood.
The rims are netless. Vines creep down the girders.

A young man aged by scars and skirmishes
walks up and down the line addressing them.
Their clothes hang off of them. They're not well fed,
these paper cutout refugees, these extras,
but one of them snaps quickly into focus.
He too is thin, pared down essentially,
the vengeance for his murdered family
alight in the cracked glaze of his hazel eyes.
The governor. His father. Kerosene glow
around the kitchen table. Old griefs surfaced
in that time of confusion and sunset darking,
electric light no longer pushing back the night.

But no. Too much like a collective dream of movies.
It's mostly about time, I try to say,
so give your people some weariness and dirt.

Remember the abandoned gas station
on a Georgia overpass this summer.
Think about rust, how Queen Anne's Lace grows best
beside a road or in abandonment.
Think about gravity, degeneration.
Store everything away for later use.
Register voices coming down the hall
against their outside ringing, all the ways
we leave this faintest living in our wake.
Let the atlas hang like a tapestry.
Lay out a stage for your fable of shades.
Given the silence, do with us what you
will there. Look closely as you do. Closer.

Apologies

First to the tow-truck driver who
helped me lift the car from its teetering
on the culvert pipe, for turning away
without asking later that evening when
my former student lay beside me finally
becalmed after the accident.
Your discreet kindness reminded me
of Whitman and was a sweet godly rebuke
as I stroked her black hair
and thought of the family I'd left.

To the cab drivers and train operators
all over Tokyo, airport personnel, too,
but especially the one with a face like
ash who held his umbrella over me,
smoking with ancient patience, unblinking,
as water ran down his face.
He knows before I do the passport is still
on my dresser, as it is every time.
Then the ride back home, wrong directions.
Am I saying *chopsticks* or *bridge*?

And for you, the two angry brothers:
I wish I could have helped after you pulled
me from the fakery of the happy family
gathered around the white pickup. The thing
you showed me twisted in the sheets—brother
or sister it was hard to say—knew me.
Though it could not speak, it has not released
me yet. Still I see the mottled hair, the skin
yellow as the cab driver's nails, a finger
rising to point at the second-hand lamp.

Martyrdom to guilt makes an arrogance.
Senators who come from trailer parks.
We nurse the survivor's passage to comfort
like a final smoke or clove on a bad tooth.

Sometimes the abandonment gets smaller
as it goes away. In the last car
of the Shinjuku Express, a hand wipes mist
from the window or maybe waves goodbye
before the tunnel swallows it. On the platform
the umbrellas go up, covering the faces.

Even Here

The rifle the truck the church the pew
the pastor the hymn the prayer
The tenor and alto soprano and bass
the dresses the cloth to bear

The savior and grace the wounds the blood
the bones the boards the splinters
The major chords yet the minor key
through which the bullet enters

The altar call the empty shells
the sheep on his good right hand
the least of these the not yet born
the haircuts the wedding bands

The thoughts the prayers the shrug the wish
the Lord and his setting sun
The bigger graves and the smaller ones
the guns the guns the guns

The Feeling

We never talk about it, or hardly ever.
It's hard enough to see it for what it is,
which is what it is not—books never written,
except the catalog copy of a life
you might massage between diaper and gin,
its wares, its fetishes, its narrative agencies:
50s sci-fi paraphernalia, espadrilles
some just for walking some for drinking,
Victorian-era piano stool wrapped
in deep-ruby velvet like a steamed bun
to complement the splashes of blood-shades
you place like motifs in a difficult text
in the apartment: dish towel, welcome
mat, cat collar. Such care and restraint
organized. Exhaustion only from spin class.
There you are in an infinity pool
in Provence, two fit strangers much like
yourself. Some subheadings:
Languor of Sunday Afternoons Neverending.
You Extoll Your Niece's Perspicacity
On the Viola to Friends with Children
Then Feel Obtuse and Sad Until
Muddling Sugar for the Second Old-Fashioned.
You Sleep the Sleep of the Trivial-Minded.
Your Delicate Porcelain Household Gods
from Thailand Survive Well into Retirement.
The Recorded Tides You Had to Yourself
Polish the Sharp Edges of Your Solitude
And No One Haggles Over Your Possessions.

Recurrences

It is the one in which my kids are gone.
It is the one in which my wife has left.
It is the one in which my ex-wife is
my now-wife and my now-wife never was.

It is the one in which I'm stuck again
in Tokyo and my passport is expired.
It is the one in which the towers fall
and I am stuck in Tokyo watching tv.

It is the one in which we all get off
the train and everyone except me walks
away and no more trains come and my ex-wife
is searching for my passport in the rubble.

It is the one in which my ex-wife is
the mother of my children and they love her.
It is the one in which the towers fall
upon the children following my ex-wife.

It is the one in which my son is lost
but no one stops to help in all of Tokyo.
It is the one in which my wife is locked
inside a tower while my daughter waves.

It is the one in which the refugees
have faces nothing like my children's faces
and yet I know they're all of them my children
more so the ones I do not recognize.

It is the one in which they dive like nymphs
into the waves to haul the boats and children
ashore, and later as I walk the beach
I peer through beach glass at their tide-rocked bodies.

It is the one in which my children climb
the tower so that I can see them wave
to me in my apartment in Tokyo
where I've been stuck for weeks amid my rubble.

It is the one in which the little backpacks
hang on their hooks and never do come down,
the names in blocky print written inside
or safely stowed behind the plastic windows.

It is the one in which their shields all fail,
when superheroes hide behind the desks,
when princesses cannot throw up a charm
to keep the monster at the castle gate.

It is the one in which my children know
they will not walk out of the cineplex
alive, the one in which they will not know
the ending of the princess and the superhero.

It is the one in which I find out which
of these are true and still I keep on dreaming.
It is the one in which I stand there thinking,
the one in which I stand there doing nothing.

Bells

He woke one morning to the sound of bells.
They kept on, as if the parish conspired
to baptize the city or the superintendent
held out hope for the one lost child.

Except there was no church or school.
He noticed many hollow things instead,
the ones he loved and those he only used.
Their many keys. The flavors of their chords.

First of the things he loved was how their breathing
filled up the rooms, or so he thought he heard.
So hard to tell when all the doors were locked,
hiding what may or may not have still lived there.

And of the things they once had used together,
the toaster sang and kept on singing,
even after he felt the sides for warmth.
The humming and the cold went up his arm.

The Burgundies keened off a kind of dirge,
hung upside down under the cabinet
and emptied of their wine like penitents,
their opened mouths a choir of Os.

But what the bells announced he couldn't say,
or why he was the only one awake
to hear them. When he finally spoke, the names
he called for struck like clappers in the dawn.

Trying to Refuse to Lament

The Buddhist in me tells me I should say
don't worry, all is change. This world of weeds,
crabgrass and thistle, pig weed and sparrows,
the melted, glassine tides of jellyfish,
we give now to you. It has been our will.
Your coral reefs are likely white as bone.
The bones of bats lie in their catacombs.
We cannot say we were not warned of this.
We can say that the glory and the strangeness,
the utter uselessness of its poetry,
were things we had no use for anymore.
What forces leached the plenty from the world,
reduced it to such sameness? Will you even notice?
Perhaps you'll see its beauty anyway.
Today I stood waist-deep in the Gulf
and saw little more than my reflection.
Here in the old earth still the baobab tree
rises in its pillared trunk through centuries
under a sidereal river trailing down
where otherwise no light shines on the plain.
See here the poisonous blue and yellow frogs
of Mexico, the fond pajamas of their skins
soon thickened like a death coat, dead as stones.
We still remember when it was hard to tell between
the beasts of the yard and the beasts of the book,
dramatis personae of a madman,
for who would bring into the light such oddments,
who take the trouble to stipple the finch's brow
or set the leaves of cottonwoods to wobble
just so? The Lord told Job to reckon with
the sky, the whale, the dragon, and the post,
but I have smaller things to tell you.
Believe me, fruit as small as those finch's eggs
once hung from plants right there, just outside the door.

Pallbearer's Privilege

I had been married four months when I tapped
my ring on the coffin. Glint of silver,
glint of chrome. I thought of a hood
and then no engine under it as Miller & Sons
unwound the winch and lowered him in.
My son would be out in the world that fall—
my wife, having come to the family
late in my life, stayed at my mother's
setting out pitchers and cold salad,
exempt from burial duty on the hill.

And so I also thought of exchanges,
one body gone, another on its way,
idle committee chit chat in the brain,
except that earlier, at the service,
the pastor, also still a farmer,
said maybe one true thing about him
but had no metaphors to offer,
only his checked shirt and a chance
for anyone inclined to stand on up
and accept Christ. I touched my wife's belly.

The fuel tank near the implement shed
made something of the same sound when you knocked.
You had to climb it first, pretending
you had some job to do that needed a stone
or the little ball-peen hammer.
Gong it went as you listened for an answer.
First the strike then the sound of its leaving.
You could tell how full or empty by its tone.
You had to put your ear right up to it
to hear the spirit in its shyness.

About the Author

Paul Bone is the author of *Nostalgia for Sacrifice* (David Robert Books) and has published poems in *The Hopkins Review, 32 Poems, The Birmingham Poetry Review, The Southern Poetry Review,* and other journals. He lives in North Texas and is Co-Editor of Measure Press.

www.ingramcontent.com/pod-product-compliance
Lightning Source LLC
Chambersburg PA
CBHW030912170426
43193CB00009BA/818